CRITICAL ACCLAIM

"In poems with a wide field of reference—art, music, poetry, myth—Eileen Thalenberg writes 'with an eye on the sacred' and on how it permeates everyday life. Here there are secret names beneath names, dark pasts behind the speaker's own past, and resonant silences where meaning emerges from restraint. *And Yet...* fills with life spaces reserved for remembering familial and historical loss and offer a sensuous 'solace of the present.'"

Roger Greenwald
author of *An Opening in the Vertical World*

"Thalenberg, a polyglot and documentarian, weaves and spins her loves in art, music, and literature. A 'requisite poet' speaks directly to our days, 'The shape of love was worry' is juxtaposed with appreciations of the ordinary: sunlight glancing off Parisian streets and the trail of chatter outside a café; waft of tangerine midst wearied workers on a city bus. Beautiful self-reflexive passages thread through Thalenberg's complex relationship to family, history, and place, elucidating an erudite struggle for grace."

Sonja Greckol
author of *Monitoring Station*

"It was the pandemic, and yet... And yet Eileen Thalenberg sat down every day and wrote a poem. Her genius was to start somewhere in the never-ending everydayness of life and end up in a place of wit and wisdom. To be in her poetic company is to spend time with a writer for whom the world opens through language, a language she not only speaks but can translate for us, so that we, too, become aware 'that the miraculous passes so close.'"

Lynda Shorten
Director, Programming, CBC Radio

I0895919

And Yet...

And Yet...

POEMS

Eileen Thalenberg

mosaic PRESS

Library and Archives Canada Cataloguing in Publication

Title: And yet... / Eileen Thalenberg.
Names: Thalenberg, Eileen, author.

Identifiers: Canadiana (print) 2025013148X | Canadiana (ebook) 20250132737 | ISBN 9781771618403 (softcover) | ISBN 9781771618434 (Kindle) | ISBN 9781771618427 (EPUB) | ISBN 9781771618410 (PDF)

Subjects: LCGFT: Poetry.
Classification: LCC PS8589.H33 A82 2025 | DDC C811/.54—dc23

Published by Mosaic Press, Oakville, Ontario, Canada, 2025.
MOSAIC PRESS, Publishers
www.Mosaic-Press.com

Design, typesetting, and cover by Lindsay Smail
This book is set in Maiola.

Printed and bound in Canada.

ONTARIO CREATES
Funded by the Government of Canada
Financé par le gouvernement du Canada
Canada

MOSAIC PRESS
1252 Speers Road, Units 1 & 2, Oakville, Ontario, L6L 2X4 (905)-825-2130
info@mosaic-press.com • www.mosaic-press.com

for my parents

CONTENTS

I Earning a Living 3
The Wrestler 4
Anansi 5
Magnificat – Washing Floors in the Time of the Pandemic 6
After Goethe, Schubert et al. 7
Next 8
Moving 9
The Yvette 11
A Taste of Spring 12
Lost in Translation 13
To the Very End 14
Stillness 15
Exile 16

II Cestello Annunciation of Sandro Botticelli 19
Not by Bread Alone 20
After Miro 21
The Floating World 22
Hokusai 23
Monet 24
Lessons I Learned from Sparrows 25

III Clocks 29
Rejected Poems 30
After Basho 31
Language of Birds 32
January 10th 33
Duet 34
Meditation 35
Berlin 36
Evening Morse 37

Found 38
Monarch Elevator Company 39
Overview 40
The Comfort of Rain 41
City Light 42
Late Afternoon 43
Vespers 44
A Sunday in Armenia 45
First Day of Autumn 46
Silence 47
Gen Gap 48

IV What's in a Name 51
Grandmothers 52
Family Lexicon 53
Easter Parade 54
If Asked 55
Siblings 56
Still Life 57
Marginalia 59
Thread 60
Lenses 61
Navalny 63
Book by Book 64
Statues of History 65
Saints & Angels 66
Streetcar 67
Long Ago 68
Indecision 69
Smoking 70
The Darkroom 72

NOTES 75
ACKNOWLEDGEMENTS 76
ABOUT THE AUTHOR 77

"and the miraculous passes so close..."
Anna Akhmatova

I

Earning a Living

It's the way the farmer bends
toward the scythe
in Van Gogh's drawing
and the gleaners in the fields
in Millet's painting
the way my father stooped over
the wooden board that was his table
stretching the pelts to ply his trade
or the carpet weavers over their yarn
or the waitress leaning over
to place dinner before me
and the way the poet hunches over
a notebook, each working
to earn a place on this earth
leaning,
embracing,
bowing before
what needs to be done.

The Wrestler

I wake exhausted.
All night I've been wrestling
– or so it seems –
with sheets, the heat,
unwelcome dreams
I no longer remember.

I think of Jacob wrestling
with his angel, and wonder
what angel visited me.
In Rembrandt's painting
the scene resembles
a locked embrace between two lovers:
the angel smiling tenderly,
Jacob, every muscle determined,
straining to win the battle.

I see how difficult
the struggle for love can be
often using force against
a door that opens inward.

Anansi

It's not Anansi weaving that web
each night on the stool where the jade plant
basks in the sun. Otherwise, I'd bargain
for a story, not sit here mutely.

I haven't caught sight of her yet
but daily fragments of silk
hang from the rungs, every
gleaming thread caught by the sun.

Each day wind tears the web apart,
each night the spider returns
to rebuild. I envy her faith as
my days hopelessly repeat.

Anansi tells me Genesis again, how
the world is recreated each moment, begins
with chaos and made into light,
sometimes simply with a breath.

Magnificat – Washing Floors in the Time of the Pandemic

Yesterday I cleaned my house
listening to Bach's Magnificat.
I can't say that my soul magnified or rejoiced
as I scrubbed the bathtub with disinfectant
washed counters with Mr. Clean
but I did pause
at the "lowly handmaiden" phrase
imagining what it would be like
to be "regarded" here,
in isolation,
without a soul to praise
or cast a critical eye,
just cleaning,
nothing more,
nothing less.

After Goethe, Schubert et al.

Like Gretchen at the spinning wheel
dreaming of love, we played spin the bottle
hoping it would stop
point to the boy we had a crush on,
the one who danced in white buck shoes
with Elvis singing Jailhouse Rock,
could swing you round the dancehall floor
and catch you when the music stopped.
At fourteen, obsessed with love and incantations:
"While twisting the stem of the apple
recite the alphabet until the stem
breaks off," and left wondering
who is this secret love that begins
with the letter "H"?
Or wishful over the innocent daisy:
"He loves me, he loves me not."
What did we know in those days,
then always hopeful
as if it were about to happen,
dreaming at the spinning wheel
waiting for the thread to grow long
enough for Love to find its way to us.

Next

a chorus of tulips open at once
summoned by an invisible maestro

their colours could start a riot,
a crowd of people stare in disbelief

the next day, unexpected heat –
the stems that hold the blooms aloft

turn soft and bend
the flowers, open-mouthed

their black tongues trembling,
swoon onto the pavement

their gasp for water, for air,
for life – so short this life...

"Next come the alums," says
the unsentimental gardener

and even as he speaks,
the arrow-headed irises

loom in the background,
not far behind

waiting their turn
for the others to retire

Moving

"You'll have to clear the clutter,"
says the real estate agent.
Clutter? I wince and look around
the rooms through his eyes,
and see what's been accumulated
thirty years in this house,
and what can't be taken when I leave.

The plants will have to go
the old hand-me-down sofa
where friends have slept throughout the years,
and complained of its discomfort,
the knick-knacks on the mantle
especially the carved fish meant as a gift
then rejected on sober second thought.

But hardest of all: the books.
Crammed shelves must be emptied
and the awful choice – which to keep
and which to pass to others
who will either read or discard.

I lay books into boxes like coffins
each one wrenches memories
of past selves. Dedications
on leaves, when and where given
and by whom come tumbling
from unknown recesses.

Between the pages a card
for my eighteenth birthday,
pressed flowers offered
by a lover long forgotten
a receipt from Les Filles du Roy
where we celebrated what?

From William Saroyan's *Human Comedy*
a letter of love and longing falls
from my mother to my brother
and his terse reply: "Thanks for the sweater
and the cookies but we're too busy
to visit next month."
What to do with these letters
from the dead to the dead?

Do snakes grieve when they shed their skin?
Oh to shed without regret, to walk away,
to step into the unknown
until the final shedding.

The Yvette

I don't know the name of the river
where Monet's boat-studio floated
but it reminds me of the languid way
the Yvette winds through Lès-Chevreuse,
where we meet every summer
and walk along the path beside the water –
two women growing older by the year.
We crisscross the twenty-two little bridges
back and forth like our conversation that has lasted
forty years about lost loves and children,
mourning the dead here and there,
gossiping about friends, remembering
with humour and with sadness mixed
and still puzzled about why's and when's.
This place is where horses
were once brought to drink,
facing the tanneries and abattoirs,
their destiny one day. Here too
the washhouses where women
kneeled on stone slabs
leaning over the water,
to scrub sheets and shirts
of the houses they served
and toward each other
to share the town's gossip
flights of swallows,
darting back and forth,
swooping for insects
above the water, catching
parts of their conversation
as they do ours this day.

A Taste of Spring

The illusion that exalts us is dearer to us
than ten thousand truths.
Anton Chekhov

Lately I see Chekhov's characters
everywhere I look.
It's the end of April
and we know how fickle it can be.
Dressed in down jackets
we sit shivering in the premature
outdoor café clutching
our coffee cups to warm our hands.
A nasty wind is blowing.
One of us is adamant: it's spring!
Dressed in a thin cotton blouse,
turquoise if I remember correctly,
she's pretending it's spring
the goosebumps on her arms
notwithstanding and her claim: "it's warm,
just a little spring breeze."
I think of Nikolai Ivanich
in Chekhov's story "Gooseberries"
tasting the hard, sour fruit
from his garden declares:
"How sweet they are."

Lost in Translation

It's only because he's drunk
that he invites me to sit
next to him, on the floor.
It's only because I speak
his language that he declares
his love for me.
He is homesick, sick of the cold,
of prose, of the prosaic, of people
who don't understand vodka
or symbols or metaphors,
he invites me to his dacha,
in the woods, describes
the birches, the small river
that runs by, such beauty
and begins to weep,
"You are the only one
who understands me."
The others in a circle
around us, wait for my
translation of the drama
at play before their eyes.
I say, "He wants to go home,"
and someone fetches the car keys
willing to oblige.

To the Very End

Auch das Schöne muss sterben
Friedrich Schiller

Whatever's dear to us
will be lost,
the dancer's leap
every year a little lower,
a polyp in the singer's throat
and the voice gives up.
At twenty-seven Beethoven
began losing his hearing
first the high notes
then the rest.
"We must learn
to die each day,"
says the Zen master
and Renoir strapped his brush
to arthritic hands
and painted to the end.

Stillness

The stillness of the pianist's hands
resting on the keyboard the moment before
first notes are sent into a hushed room.

The withdrawal into the silent space,
the audience holding their breath,
never more attentive

than in this moment before,
both prepare for the music to enter
both listen for the beginning.

Like the diver poised to entrust
body to air and water,
the mind composed,

all muscles taut as strings
and then an in-breath
before release.

It is said that God too prepared
before the beginning and withdrew
in an infinite contraction

making space for creation,
and then exhaled, life breathed
into all that was born.

Exile

I try to imagine what it was like for them,
the nameless ones, to leave the garden,
after the booming voice of the boss
and all the curses, to be driven
ignominiously out of Eden,
not allowed to take a thing along.
Was there a gate unseen that suddenly appeared,
an archway with those nasty noisy cherubim
overhead and the fiery sword revolving
as if in a discotheque? Or was it like
a sci-fi movie: whoosh, the background
suddenly changes, they look around
in disbelief and "Wow! What the hell
just happened?" Instead of standing
in the garden, they're on a road
with no signs marking where they are,
nothing to tell them where to go,
and not a living soul to ask.

II

Cestello Annunciation of Sandro Botticelli

The room resembles any other in 1489:
terra cotta tiles on the floor,
a spacious room, through the window
a distant landscape, a tree, a river –
the promised land? The stage is set.
A visitor arrives with news.
It's the angel Gabriel and we understand
what he has been sent to tell the woman
who turns away from him in fear
not out of startle but because
she knows that every angel is a terror.
Mary wants no part of it,
she has forgotten her line:
"Let it be done." She flees
from the angel, "No thank you,"
she seems to be saying,
foreshadowing her son's words:
"Take this cup from me."
Botticelli must have been suspicious
of these intermediaries,
bearers of no great gifts,
who either "pour out bowls of God's wrath"
or make impossible demands.

Not by Bread Alone

Two black dots for eyes
a zig-zag line – the mouth
all encircled with a thin line
what else does a human being need?
Perhaps a few elliptical lines
for tufts of hair
and voilà – there it is!
"But a person needs more,"
I say to Miro, "stars, a moon..."
"Of course," he says
and adds a bird.

After Miro

I

Dogs can't go up ladders
but a man can climb
as far as the ladder goes.
The dog is barking
at the man in the moon
begging him, come back
not to leave him in the dark
alone on the earth.

II

On the totem a gnarled finger
emerges from a mouth
as if the words need emphasis.
A wise toad sits on the head
keeping silence.

III

A mouth, surrounded by night,
opens in surprise
listening to stars
gossiping.

The Floating World

In the painting there are men and women
carrying something or someone:

a mother with an infant in her arms
a father, his child on his shoulders
a woman balancing two baskets of food
hung from a bamboo stick on her neck

what you see is ordinary life
borne not as burden
but out of love

before your eyes
three are cooking on an open fire
stirring noodles into a cauldron
a woman weaves while breastfeeding
someone is hanging laundry

all around is water
and everywhere are children
peeking around corners, watching
swimming – water babies like cherubs

and of course, somewhere in their midst
a few curious dogs, some colourful birds
and two requisite poets reciting aloud
some people are listening
and others are not

Hokusai

Thirty-six times Hokusai drew Mt. Fuji,
carved each view into woodblocks
and set the images to paper.
In each the mountain
sits like a Buddha, witness
to the busyness of human life.
The fishermen cast their rods
into the river, people wash laundry,
fly kites. There's a barrel maker,
water-carriers, carpenters, and even a man
who stops to tie his sandal on the road.
Whether at temple or watermill,
daily tasks are attended, all with an eye
on the sacred, the still-point in their midst.

Monet

Day after day Monet gazed at his neighbour's haystacks
watched the light change as it changed them
morning light, noon, the oblique light
of magic hour in late afternoon
and then sunset.
He painted them in autumn's flame
and spring's mist, their peaks capped
in winter snow, the very air
as the seasons cycled
through the year.
The theme repeated was the haystack,
the variation – the light.
Twenty-five canvasses in all.
He was in his 50s
trying to capture
the moment vanishing,
time itself.

Lessons I Learned from Sparrows

1. The sparrow flies by resisting gravity

2. If it weren't for birds we'd never look up

3. Sing even though you're invisible

4. Sing the few notes you've been allotted

5. Take baths often, even when there is only a bit of water

III

Clocks

For a child time has no meaning,
with every clock she draws,
time stops.

When I'm gone no one will remember
the clock that ticked
in the white kitchen of my childhood
its face bursting out
from the centre's golden metal rays.

There, I've made time stand still.

Rejected Poems

Think of them as homing pigeons
or wounded animals
coming back for comfort.

After Basho

I climb uphill through the ravine
to improve my heart rate.
Ah! the forsythia.

Language of Birds

crows on the wire
commas
in a run-on sentence

January 10th

curbsides piled with mattresses
waiting for the trash collectors
January the biggest month for divorce

Duet

The crack in the window
whistles one note
waiting for its harmonic

Meditation

seven seated round a silent pool
fishing

Berlin

Dark at half past three
impatient to flaunt its Christmas lights
a blue and yellow Pegasus,
trees wreathed in glowing ornaments
golden angels
and a Star of David peering out
from behind the Brandenburg Gate.

Evening Morse

5 p.m.
the black clouds pinned to the sky
all afternoon are subsumed
into night.

Lights go on one by one
dots and dashes, here and there,
messages in evening code:
I'm home, I'm here,
I'm waiting for you.

Found

a pair of ballet shoes
in fifth position
forsaken on an empty lawn –
an abandoned dream?
a rebellion?

Monarch Elevator Company

The sign on the one-storey building:
High Hopes for Business
but can you trust an elevator company
that's never risen above
a ground-floor office?

Overview

Three tall sunflowers, their heads
bent over the balcony rail
watch as I walk by
and I think of the old ladies in Paris,
chores done, dinner in the oven,
leaning out the window to see
what's happening in the street.
Food for gossip later on.

The Comfort of Rain

on tin roofs
on skylights now clouded

rain skips on cobblestones
in the courtyard below

two bicycles glisten, lean
against carved wooden doors
waiting.

City Light

There's a way the sun
glides along the cream-coloured walls,
and limestone buildings of Paris
on streets large and small
glow with a warm light.

People walk about
as if wearing haloes
the sun shining through
their hair.

Here on rue Verlomme
that ends in Café Janou
there's always a hopeful clutch
of young men and women waiting
for a table, and light sweeps slowly by
leaving the darkening street
with a trail of chatter
and laughter.

Late Afternoon

Wind chimes in the garden
perfume of rose and lavender
the sound of water splashing
in the stone fountain, a hummingbird
has come for her evening shower.
In the distance a dog is barking.

I sit in a triangle of sunlight
soon the Earth will turn me away
toward a night sky
perhaps some stars, perhaps not
it's never guaranteed.

Vespers

Evening vespers of birds
and the last of the day's light
glistening on autumn trees
draw me out.
From a neighbour's window
Brahms cello sonata
pours into the street.
Strange, this music
familiar
now catches me
by surprise,
so much yearning
passes through me
left wondering
where does the music go after?

A Sunday in Armenia

The happy wedding party
is skipping up the stairs
to the church in Yerevan,
only the goat being pulled
by a rope is reluctant,
his cries meh-meh-meh
pierce the general laughter
he knows he is the only sacrifice
that God will provide today.

First Day of Autumn

Remembering their cue
orange and gold boldly make an entrance
as if they couldn't keep their secret
any longer.

I know that feeling.

As a child, my mother's birthday gift in hand
I couldn't wait for it to be unwrapped
just to see the look on her face.

Silence

We were talking about silence
and each had a story about it
how sorry we were,
yes, each said how sorry they were,
that there's no room for it
these days. And so it went.

Gen Gap

Things are changing too quickly, she says,
names, gender, borders
everything has become so fluid
it's hard to keep up.
"Whatever," says the teenager
sailing past,
leaving her behind.

IV

What's in a Name

Christina, my mother pulled that name
from the most remote place
her mind could reach
a name to least betray me
should the need arise
one the nuns would love
"die kleine Christlein" they whispered
over me like a benediction
in the Frauenklinik in Linz.
But underneath another name
a secret code was breathed:
Chaya, life, resurrecting
her own mother
who did not survive.

Grandmothers

Visiting the old toothless grandmother
Not mine but a New World substitute,
The ritual Sunday excursion.
Adults standing solemnly around her bed
Her dry voice still with the power to command
Crackled in the airless room.
My secret place was on the low white bench
Beneath the rubber tree plant,
The white cat substituting for a tiger.
Adult voices interrupt
I wonder where did all the grandmothers go,
Was the hairless one in the other room
the last one left...

Family Lexicon

our sincerest laughter
with some pain is fraught
Percy Bysshe Shelley

When was the word "joy" struck
from our family lexicon?
It contained "celebration"
but there was no joy.
There were "candles" but always
accompanied by tears
that threatened to dampen the flame
a sigh that made it shiver
and sometimes snuffed it out.
My father would say "remember,"
my mother "don't forget."
Room for losses
always revived,
who was missing and why,
afraid to praise, afraid of pride,
afraid of the evil eye.
And there were other entries
for "fear"
for "hiding"
in that order.

Easter Parade

Easter morning. The air fills
with the sound of bells ringing from churches
behind Esplanade Avenue, strikes fear
into the hearts of its Jewish immigrants,
memories of pogroms, forced conversions
run like ancient rivers through their veins,
generate instinctive waves of panic.

But we children love a parade.
The head priest in his gold-trimmed
cassock and mitre, followed by black-clad
priests with red beanies (we called them yarmulkehs),
the smell of incense trailing after them
down the street, the huge wooden cross
held aloft – empty, no sign of the tortured figure
we've seen on other crosses.

Everyone seems happy, perhaps
we should be too. Now that he's risen
maybe the Catholic kids will stop
yelling *maudit juif*, blaming us
for killing their hero.

Back on the street it's cops and robbers,
our heroes Roy Rogers, Wyatt Earp,
the cap-gun smell of sulphur
permeates the air. "Bang, bang!
You're dead!" "No I'm not!"

If Asked

the shape of love was worry
its depth, and breadth
everything it touched
some would call it prayer

Siblings

We never saw eye to eye
though born
of the same mother and father
I belonged "there," the old country
you were of "here."
You remembered love
I remembered fear,
and both were right

Still Life

I

Amo, amas, amat,
My mother's head leans over me
The black Latin grammar lies on my lap
As the pots sizzle on the stove.
Amo, amas, amat,
I repeat the words by rote
While my mother kneads the dough
For the Sabbath bread.

II

You need to shell peas
In the kitchen
To earn the stories
One by one

III

She wore her busyness like a carapace all week
Monday laundry, Tuesday ironing, mending,
And always there were pots
Sweating on the stove,
Children to be worried into a future
And a husband – an unreliable provider.
Wednesday, Thursday, relentlessly
One after the other
And always the question will there be enough
Friday, breads were kneaded, strudel dough held aloft
Spread paper-thin on fingertips.
But came a moment
When the week tumbled into stillness.

The lace kerchief on her head
The Sabbath candles lit,
She raised her hands above the flames, sighed
And gathered the light to her self.

IV

The crisscrossed needles
Sit idly in the skein of wool
Like hands folded
When work is done.
She's been gone
More than twenty years
And the half-finished scarf
Meant for me
Waits to be completed.
She never taught me how to knit,
Those were her private moments.
I look at perfect, even rows
And wonder
What secret desires were remembered
And how many demons
Cast off stitch by stitch.

Marginalia

I begin to worry:
only a few pages left in my notebook.
It's not that paper is expensive
but the place where I shop
"Closed Due to Plague."
I will have to start writing
in the margins, not as ancient scribes
annotating or decorating the perimeter
of manuscripts and scrolls,
but as my mother did
in the three notebooks she had
while hidden in a closet in 1943 –
her handwriting small, and smaller,
framed each page – like Voltaire
composing in the margins of books
while in prison, like Sir Walter Raleigh
just before his execution, each
in their own way, writing
against the dark.

Thread

When I enter my father's room, I hear
"I want to go..." but where?
The word won't come.
He rubs forefinger against thumb
as if pulling thread from a spool whose end
he hopes will summon the missing word,
feeding thread onto spindle
to be spun into language.
With thumb against forefinger
he can remember how it feels
but no sound appears.
Long years of practice
pulling and feeding threads
through a lifetime of labour,
soon draw the word he now recalls:
"Home. I want to go home."
A cry heard at both ends of life.

Lenses

A small black leather pouch
holds two lenses ground
from Russian vodka bottles
during the last world war.
They were once my father's
glasses, the kind that Isaac Babel
or Trotsky would have worn.
He claimed they were
the best he'd ever had
and put them in my hands
to show how light they were.

He had a clear view of a world at war,
the plundering and the kindnesses
profiteering and generosity,
through the lens of one place
called Archangelsk.
The reindeer-lined boots of Stalin's
emissaries, the sausages and vodka
visible from their fur coat pockets,
local children gathering kindling
from garbage heaps to take home,
and what was easily bought and sold
if one had the right currency,
sometimes it was love
not the sordid kind, a fair exchange,
the kind that comforts
a woman whose husband
is fodder at the front

and warms a soldier whose wife's
two-year silence is unbearable.

Through those lenses
there is no looking back
nor any view to the future,
a temporary home life is made.
The solace of the present,
impermanent though it is,
was all that could be seen
and that became enough.

Navalny

Time for a requiem
no need for a new one,
the old one will suffice.

What else is there to do
but turn to Akhmatova
where Russia still "writhes
beneath blood-stained boots."

Book by Book

You'd think dictionaries are impartial,
what could be simpler:
a word and its definition,
sometimes many definitions,
sometimes one is dropped,
leaves you wondering why, because
you remember once when it was there.
Sometimes whole words disappear
like people in Stalin's Russia,
sometimes rehabilitated,
sometimes not.
Sometimes whole books disappear
the smell of pages burning, the flames
licking commas, colons, sentences, ideas,
almost the same odour of book banning,
in Iran, Afghanistan, US of A, no one is immune
to history's monotonous repetition.
"There are worse crimes than burning books,"
wrote Joseph Brodsky. "One of them is not reading them."

Statues of History

There goes Stalin, and Robert E. Lee,
Enver Hoxha and Christopher Columbus
kings, czars, and generals beheaded or pulverized,
Ryerson and Rhodes stripped of stature,
schools, streets renamed, words expunged
from books, from mouths – erase the evils of history.
And history? It slithers snake-like in the underbrush,
insinuating itself between blades of grass, waits,
lifts its prehistoric head and flicks a thin red tongue.
The snake sheds its skin many times, yet remains a snake.

Saints & Angels

It takes so little to be a saint these days –
a friend desperate for a forgotten phone number
asks can I find it please.

I send her the ten digits
she texts me back: "You're a saint"
I have it here in plain English

in Helvetica type on my phone.
Easier than all the popes in line
for sainthood.

Google tells me that canonization
depends on martyrdom or miracles,
unfortunately, the first step
to become a saint is to die.

My mother used to call me an "angel"
I'm not sure which is worthier
in the hierarchy of beings.

Someone who once wished her dead
said: "Ah, she is already among the angels."
So, angel or saint, either way,
death is a prerequisite.

Streetcar

Through the damp odour rising from woolen caps
and fur collars slicked back with melting snow,
through the crush of workers emptied out
from factories at five, now packed into the trolley car,
and children clutched by weary mothers worried
if dinner will be on the table by six
how to keep a balance
not tumble on the man behind –
the scent of a tangerine opened
hangs in the air for a moment
then descends like a blessing.

Long Ago

the ancients drew lines from star to star,
birds and wingèd horses were created,
virgins and hunters made visible,
fixed in the heavens,
relationships mirrored on earth.
Today we no longer believe
the stories the night skies once told.
Nor have we invented new ones.
This silence, this space
is all that remains
emptying into darkness –
and immeasurable sadness
that you and I could not imagine
ourselves into the stars.

Indecision

The room has darkened while you wait patiently
for an answer to a question asked hours ago
or was it years? – the glow from your cigar
steadily on and off,
a beacon beckoning me ashore.
We sit among shadows growing
in silence, our breathing – a fugue,
one of us softly tapping a pulse,
all is rhythm now –
"It's your move," you say.

Smoking

First the unmistakable smell,
then nostalgia...
someone on the street
is smoking.
Once in my rented attic room
looking out the window
I glimpsed my reflection
lost in thought, smoking,
the glamour of it,
Simone Signoret
in *Room at the Top.*
It's been almost thirty years
since the last cigarette
the romance of a Gauloise
in my hand, smoke rings
curling back to cafés
thick with the fog of smoke
making all conversation
intimate.
The scent of smoke
on a man's jacket
as he takes it off
tosses it on the chair
beside the bed.
The glow of two cigarettes
eyes on fire
against the night sky
as we lay in the field
in search of Venus.

Those were the days
a cigarette was enough
to introduce you
to a handsome stranger:
"Excuse me, do you have a light?"

The Darkroom

There we were in the darkroom
delighted with the day's photographs
emerging in the bath trays
like the world after an eclipse.
Then the phone rang.
In the glow of the red safe light
I glimpsed a certain look on your face
– the deception visible at last in black and white –
opened the door into the light
and never looked back.

p. 5: Anansi references a character from West African and Caribbean folklore known as a storyteller associated wisdom, knowledge, and trickery, most commonly depicted as a spider.

p. 12: Reference to Anton Chekhov's short story *Gooseberries.*

p. 14: From *Die Nänie* by Friedrich Schiller.

p. 19: "Every angel is a terror" is an allusion to Rainer Maria Rilke's First Elegy of *The Duino Elegies*: "every angel is terrifying."

p. 53: Percy Bysshe Shelley from *To a Skylark.*

p. 63: The line "writhes beneath boots" is a quote from Anna Akhmatova's *Requiem*.

p. 64: Words spoken by Joseph Brodsky at the Library of Congress, Washington, 17 May 1991 on his becoming poet laureate of the United States.

ACKNOWLEDGEMENTS

A few of the poems in the book have previously been published in *Juniper Poetry Journal.*

Special thanks to Bernice Eisenstein, artist and editor par excellence, for her discerning eye and ear in helping prepare the manuscript, and especially for friendship.

In remembrance of Martha Heyneman for writing sessions over many years with encouragement to "write without apologies."

And for Rubem Fonseca (1925–2020) who knew before I did that there would be a book of poems.

ABOUT THE AUTHOR

Eileen Thalenberg is an award-winning documentary filmmaker, poet and literary translator. For many years she was writer and producer at CBC's *The Nature of Things* and later with Gail McIntyre founded the independent film and television company Stormy Nights Productions. Stormy Nights produced a variety of documentaries – from arts to political issues – that were distributed around the world and won numerous national and international awards.

Fluent in seven languages, her translations of prose, poetry and plays have been published and performed in major theatres in Canada and abroad. *The Suicide* by Nikolai Erdman translated and adapted together with Alan Richardson (Mosaic Press) was performed at The Shaw Festival Theatre and by other companies in North America. Her translations of poetry and prose have appeared in various literary journals, and her own poems most recently in *Juniper Poetry Magazine*. She has also published a book of visual poems called *Gesture Poems* (Mosaic Press).